On The Bright Side 3

Andrew Aldred

chipmunkapublishing
the mental health publisher

Andrew Aldred

All rights reserved, no part of this publication may be reproduced by any means, electronic, mechanical photocopying, documentary, film or in any other format without prior written permission of the publisher.

>
> Published by
> Chipmunkapublishing
> United Kingdom

http://www.chipmunkapublishing.com

Copyright © 2018 Andrew Aldred

ISBN   978-1-78382-406-9

Dedicated

To Jane

Andrew Aldred

Post-Election Chaos

The conservatives have forged links with the DUP
Costing the tax-payer a billion pounds so we hear
They are dependent on a backward set of Orangemen
For the final ten votes that will pass their policies
Well, at least they are getting something done
Even if it is a dirty, corrupt old business
Damn it! They are politicians, after all
Jeremy Corbyn doesn't realise he's lost the election
He's sacking people for voting against the party line
He doesn't want his party to have ideas of their own
And I think it will be to his detriment in the long run
If the Labour party is a dictatorship what will the country be?
If they get into power which they probably will
If this government cannot somehow get the country in order
And capitalise on the narrow margin they had in the election
There needs to be more room for compromise
On both sides of the political pendulum
Corbyn and May need to settle their differences
And start working together for the good of the nation

Andrew Aldred

Grenfell Tower Disaster

A whole series of failures in safety
And shortcuts in producing cheap housing
Resulted in this appalling tragedy
As usual they want to make someone responsible
That's the mob mentality for you
It's like Hillsborough all over again
And that's so sad for everyone involved
All they can give anybody is compensation
Nobody can put a price on life
The dead will not come back
My heart goes out to the people who died
Burned to death in each other's arms
Nothing could be more horrific
And for the survivors, I'm so sorry
At least something is being done now
To make tower blocks safer and more habitable
It's an event that shook the nation
At least we've learned something from it

Lost Life

It's all about one little boy
Laid out on a hospital bed with brain damage
And his parents who cannot let go
Of his precious little life
It's so understandable and so tragic
Everyone from the pope to Donald Trump is involved
It's on the news every other day
Everything being dragged through court again
Doesn't anyone trust Great Ormond Street hospital?
Does there have to be all these court battles?
The parents must have died a dozen times
Over all the attention and discord
All that was ever important was their son
And not the media circus that climbed on board
The tragic journey to him losing his life

Andrew Aldred

What's Left

She said she'd like to work in the community
But voluntary work is all we'd be fit for
And I told her they'd only take advantage of us
And not give us very much of anything back
We might as well do something for ourselves
For her daughter and our grandchild
We should try to enjoy ourselves
Like the rest of the bastards do
While they complain about us and how we carry on
Who knows how long we've got left to live?

Go Whistle for it

So, you want a hundred billion pounds
To get us out of a situation we don't want to be in
Then you want to sell us everything we need to live
I think you've overvalued yourselves
The rest of the world produces fuel, vehicles and everything else
We don't need to trade with Europe
We can demand our freedom or just take it
I'm so sorry Mr Junkers, but I haven't got the time
We've paid you a lot of money to date
We're out now. There's no deal. Sod off!

Sink Like a Stone

Some people don't want to go quietly
They want to make a stand and a big fuss
I don't see the point
When my time comes I'll just drop dead
I'll sink like a stone into the next world
And never worry about this one again

Usain Bolt

It was meant to be the last great race
And Usain Bolt was meant to win it
To complete his golden legacy forever
To everyone's amazement he came third
His face looked worn and haggard
He pulled out with cramp in the relay
Maybe if he'd taken drugs he would have won
But even the greatest of us get past our sell-by date
The man who won the hundred metres was a drugs cheat
I guess that says a lot about the way sport is going

Andrew Aldred

Pull the Plug

Does anybody want an unstable China?
Does anybody want South Korea to be obliterated?
Does anybody want a war between North Korea and the USA?
I think the answer is a resounding "No!"
The stakes are far too high
America and North Korea both need to back down
I don't care if North Korea becomes a nuclear state
Provided they don't use the weapons
Which is a lot to ask given the way they've been performing
America needs to listen to China and Russia
It is time to de-escalate this whole thing
I'm as sick of the paranoia as everyone else
What is the alternative? Half the world going up in smoke?
Life's hard enough and war can wait!

Growing Old Together

We've both tried our best for some sort of career
Only to end up ill and out of work
We've tried getting divorced and going our separate ways
We've tried to drink and smoke for years
Everything got too much for us
We've got rid of the friends we had
They never did us any good
All we've got is each other and some family
The rest of them are sick of us
And by some process of elimination
We've ended up growing old together

Andrew Aldred

Short of Inspiration

When you've written hundreds of poems
About many events in your own life
And many of the triumphs and tragedies of this world
Sometimes you struggle to find anything new
Anything exciting or refreshing
We're all looking for creativity
But it's just an endless cycle
The world carries on repeating itself
In different ways through different people
Is there anything that hasn't been written about?
I need something to come and blow me away
And then at least I'll be able to write about something new
But I can't even begin to think what on earth it will be!

Insignificant?

I wonder what anyone will think of my poems
In fifty or a hundred years' time
Will they say my poems were the work of a lunatic?
Or some great work of literature?
I wouldn't really like to speculate
It could be all too depressing
But I have been of some value to some things
And to some of the people I have known
There's some people I'm glad I have met
None of them have been public figures
Or movie stars, pop stars or anything important
They have managed to have something in common with me
And I've fallen in love at least once
I'm no less significant than a lot of people

Andrew Aldred

Bloody Useless

They're all trying to sell me things I don't want
From an amazon firestick to elixir
Some verbally driven device that controls the home
Even I can get out of my chair to do something
If I am at all awake or coherent
I've got more than a hundred channels on my TV
And I'm damned if I can be bothered to watch the news
Let alone the rest of the crap
They want me to have a car without a key
That can park itself. Have some faith in my driving!
I haven't had a crash for two years now!
I wish the boffins could invent something for me
But they reached the sum of that twenty years ago
I don't suppose they could make everything cheaper
And maybe a bit like it was in the past
Then maybe everything I buy wouldn't be second-hand

Blood Test

It's been a year now
Since I had a fit in hospital
Whilst giving blood
I've got a phobia of needles
And this event made it worse
But I'm still alive this year
And it's time for my medical
I'm going to give blood
And somehow conquer the fear
My heart races as the needle sinks in
I didn't lose consciousness
I didn't throw a fit
I can breathe easy for another year

Failed Diplomacy

Donald Trump addressed the United Nations today
He put America's position to the world very clearly
He said he would obliterate North Korea
He has backed himself into a corner
He went back on President Obama's deal with Iran
He said that all their nation brought to the middle east was chaos
The American president is not building a bridge over troubled waters
I know he is trying to face down a lunatic in the North Korean dictator
I know he believes in a white Christian god and not a Muslim one
I know that the diplomacy of the United Nations has failed
But I fear a fire is burning and he wants to fan the flames
I think if there ever was a need for diplomacy to work it is now
And I really hope Donald Trump knows what he is doing

Lads

I see them all over the place
Working class lads with attitude problems
They talk about me like I wasn't there in the local shop
They all think they're so important
But I don't see it their way
I don't believe in a community where I don't fit in
I don't believe in people I'd rather not know
I don't see any social equality anywhere
These people all want to put themselves in charge
And they think that I should do their bidding
Sorry if I'm so disappointing to you
But my life is just as important as anyone else's
And if I choose to be an outcast because I don't like what you offer
I'm fifty-one years old and I've earned the right

Andrew Aldred

Pray for Us

First there was Irma and then Maria
The latest typhoons and hurricanes
Wrecking the states of Florida and Texas
And laying waste to the Virgin Islands and Dominica
It only goes to show you're not even safe in a tropical paradise
You can have everything, and nature still comes into play
They asked us to pray for them
And when you face the wrath of God
Pray is all you can do. I hope it did some good
I hope everyone's prayers lessened the blow

Flat Tyre

I went outside today to find another flat tyre on my car
It's only three weeks since the last one
It's all too much of a coincidence
And my partner and myself suspect sabotage
But there are no obvious suspects
We only know we are disabled and of mixed race
It's not an awful lot for the police to go on
All I hope is that the stupid bastard stops wasting my time
Because I've got other things to do and to spend my money on

Loose, Wild and Wonderful

I took the bobble out of her hair last night
As she lay in my arms, asleep
When I had to move I told her I had taken it
And she said her hair was loose, wild and wonderful
I remember those days when we were all of that
When we used to talk about hot, raw sex in the pub
And fell about laughing at everyone's embarrassment
I tell myself, "We're the same, just older"
As I leave her to sleep and come downstairs
We will always be loose, wild and wonderful to each other
And we will love each other more as time goes on

Catch a Falling Star

Catch a falling star and put it in your pocket
Never let it fade away
Don't let the stampede beat you
If you want pole position, you'll have to fight for it
You'll have to get on the internet
You'll have to tour endless venues
Repeating your verses and promoting your work
Everyone wants to be a poet these days
It's easier than working on a building site
Not that every poet I've ever met could do that
I've got my excuses for being a poet
I've been reduced to a level where I can't do anything else
They won't give a mentally ill person a decent job
Even if they had the drive, energy and enthusiasm
If you want to catch a falling star
And put it in your pocket
You'd better be prepared to persevere
If you want to save it for a rainy day

Andrew Aldred

I'd Better be Alright

I guess things have turned full circle now
I've come out about my mental illness
And you've let me down gently for years
Still I remember some good times
Amongst all the tears and the pain
I'm at peace with myself and on my own
With my girlfriend as my only support
At least I've got someone I can be with
And a situation I belong in
If I can't be alright now I never will be
I have made sense of my madness

Better off Apart

Sometimes people take advantage a little too much
There should be a line drawn in the sand
With some well-established boundaries
I don't like people who set themselves up as perfect
Thinking they're living some sort of idyllic life
That they're somehow different from everyone else
When I finally began to pick fault with these people
The response was so pitifully inadequate
It's so sad that these are the people in charge
I'm never going back to prison or mental hospital
I'm tired of fighting to get a fair hearing
I'll take what little I've earned and leave them alone

Andrew Aldred

Beginnings of Abuse

Abuse starts at school and within social circles
If people can't keep it in check it snowballs
Victims get misled and fall in with the wrong crowd
They get pushed around and misused
It is then that bad things happen
If they don't take it out on themselves
They take it out on the abusers
Beware of what happens to you at school and at with your peers
It can set you off on the wrong path
And leave you with very little hope of anything better

Two-faced Bitch

I reversed into her stepdad's car
And initially she was nice as pie
She said I'd hear nothing further about the incident
Which had left a little rough paint on her car
About the size of a penny that would have polished out
But two weeks afterwards she's claiming personal injury
Neck and back pain for a collision that hardly happened
And I'm phoning the insurers every five minutes
Trying to sort things out and put the record straight
You can never trust a pretty, lying blonde girl
They see an opportunity and their eyes light up
With pound signs and money madness
That's a night out and a pair of ear-rings for me!
Don't you ever worry about the truth, love
I hope your next insurance bill costs you dearly
Because the insurers can add up as well
And they will see a lying, cheating two-faced bitch

Andrew Aldred

Catalonian Catastrophe

They've had a bogus election in Catalonia
The people there think they can do as they please
But when all is said and done that's only half the people
The other half wants to remain in Spain
There was never a proper election
Just some flag-waving that will turn into chaos
Catalonia is not recognised by anybody
There are no borders and no constitution
The people responsible are a set of idiots
They should at least have had a democratic vote
And that legally needed to include all Spaniards
It also needed to include all Catalonians
What will the aftermath be? Blood on the streets?
And potentially a lot of people thrown in jail
If you want an independent country, you do it
Through legal and constitutional means for it to be valid
This was an exercise in wasted time and effort

The Hatred in Heavy Metal

I got into rock music in the late nineteen seventies
There were classic bands like Sabbath, Zeppelin and Deep Purple
Followed by the New Wave of British Heavy Metal
And great American bands like Aerosmith and Van Halen
But as these bands progressed into the nineteen nineties
There was a new sound, taking all the worst elements of the genre
Preaching death, hatred, Satanism and violence
Pioneered by Metallica, Slayer and Megadeth
Heavy Metal has never been the same since
It is a sad sign of the times in which we live
Endless recession and little hope of a good future
Has left a lot of people very disillusioned
Everyone is an outcast these days, not just the Hells Angels
The Satanic, death/hate metal has given way
To a set of kids pissed off with life
Looking up to the likes of Kurt Cobain and Metallica
The hatred in heavy metal is here to stay

Andrew Aldred

Losing Friends

Sometimes things come to a head
Relationships get bent too far out of shape
People need to get on by themselves
For the greater good of the rest of us
First you fall out and then you try to get on the phone
And realise you are the one making all the effort
You begin to see the light over your so-called friendship
It was all on the other person's terms
You gave too much and got too little
It's such a pity when these are the people you've trusted
But when people have their own priorities and agendas
Even the closest friendships can unravel

Decline of a Dictator

He's served as a politician for five decades
Using every trick to hold on to power
Surviving numerous assassination attempts
Spending time in prison and avoiding execution
He's had a hell of a good run of luck
But his country has declined in economic terms
It is corrupt beyond belief and there's no-one to blame
Only a leader that has been ousted by the military
He thought his second wife would take over from him
But she's a disgrace and nobody wants her
It's a lonely place at the top of the heap
And there's a very long way to fall
Robert Mugabe is too old to rule a country
That went to the dogs twenty years ago

Andrew Aldred

Not That Good

I saw a hero coach-driver on the news today
Who saved an entire coachload of people from death
By sacrificing his own life and driving into a head-on collision
And I wonder "Would I be able to do that?"
I opted not to take responsibility for something today
I've been screwed often enough, and I didn't want to take the blame
It seems everyone has taken advantage of me recently
And realise I'm no hero and sometimes not very upstanding
Some people are so genuinely good it makes me want to cry
But I'm certainly not one of them all the time
Other people are so sickly in their efforts to do good
That it makes me cringe when they parade themselves on television
I'm not exactly a villain but I'm no hero
I'll do someone a favour it I can and it's not going to kill me
I take my hat off to the hero coach driver
And wish him well in the next life because I'm not that good

Things are Alright

Sometimes we go over the past
And we have the same argument all over again
There's history, herstory, and there's the truth
But all we really know is things are better now
You don't drink any more, and I drink less
We both have our own separate houses
And we've got time to miss each other
You're not going out on your own
And I don't have to worry about where you've been
We're fulfilling our obligations to our families
We're staying well and out of hospital
We shouldn't make problems. Things are alright

Andrew Aldred

Shambles

Parliament today has never been such a shamble
Everybody wants their say and there's no compromise
If we don't get some sort of order Brexit will never happen
And we will lose out in every respect
Europe is sick of in-fighting British politicians
And so am I and most of the rest of the country
Can't we just buckle down and get things done?
Is argue until we're blue in the face all we're any good at?
I'd still say the Tories are a better option than Corbyn
He would just compromise the country at every opportunity
Everybody needs to get behind Theresa May
And help to steer this country into safer waters
I hope they can work things out in the national interest

Heaven is Here

I look around and realise things will never get any better
I hold her asleep in my arms and hope it lasts
Everybody is still alive and there's nothing too wrong in our lives
We no longer work, and we've got enough money
None of us are short of a roof and we don't have to go to a food bank
I am still able to drive and keep my car on the road
Our grandson is growing up into a young man
This is our heaven and hell can wait for a long time

Andrew Aldred

Put it Down to Experience

So, you tried to do something different in the last election
And you voted for Donald Trump
It's so easy to see from a distance
How he has divided your country
Whilst he gives money to the corporations
And takes it from the poor
Well, you're stuck with him for three more years
It's a bitter pill to swallow, a hard lesson to learn
Donald Trump always was the king of bullshit
A corporate criminal out to line his own pockets
He was never about creating wealth
Only about exploiting what was already there
But after being the American president he has nothing left
Only his day job of being a corporate crook
It's so transparent. And you fell for it. God bless America!

Rat Running in a Race

I'm just a rat running in a race
I'll do nearly anything to save my face
Keep out of trouble. You know I will
I know the drill. I take my pills
I can't afford to be a clown
I don't want to get down
With the rest of them in town
Everything is designed to depersonalise
It's a society I despise
Built on criminality and lies
Everyone is getting less money
They go to food banks
To feed themselves and their family
I'm not fit to work
But I feel the need to get a job
It doesn't pay to be a slob
What on earth can I do?
Apart from write this poetry for you
I'm just a rat running in a race
Trying to save face while I live in disgrace!

Andrew Aldred

Not a Well Man

Sometimes I've got to be on my own
I can worry myself to death alone
The department of work and pensions is cutting my money
And I've got car insurance and a mortgage to pay
In this day and age you've got to prioritise
My partner is trying to enjoy our time together
But I'm paranoid beyond belief
About every little thing in our lives
We balance each other out but sometimes I need the space
My medication is affecting my vision
I need it, but I can't stand the damn stuff
There's no way they'll give me Valium
The psychiatrist doesn't even want to see me
Cancer and paranoia aren't such a great combination
The more ill I get the less the doctor wants to know
Give me some money! I'm not a well man!

The New Enemy

We've had communism against democracy
Muslims fighting the jihad against the west
Homosexuals and the Lesbian Gay Transgender revolution
Global warming and the loss of trees in the rainforests
Two antichrists and numerous wars
This is supposed to be an age of racial equality
But it all just seems to go on and on
What are they going to invent for us to face next?
Will the ice caps disappear without trace?
Will the population soar out of control?
Will the sun stop burning and explode one day?
It's all going on before our eyes and we do very little
The new enemy is the same as the old one!

Andrew Aldred

Jeremy Kyle

He makes a program for the dregs of the nation
To watch and star in
To parade their sad lives for everyone to see
The thieves, liars and love cheats
He re-unites the lost and lonely
It is fascinating viewing for my girlfriend and myself
I am frequently shocked and sometimes moved to tears
It is a morally sound program that makes something out of nothing
It sends people to rehab and gives them counselling
While Jeremy gives the naughty ones of us a telling off
I am genuinely impressed with Jeremy Kyle

The Demise of a Superpower

America is no longer the world's policeman
Or the great style guru it once was
There are two reasons for this. Donald Trump and poverty
The rest of the world wants to hold North Korea to account
All Donald Trump does is bluster
There are sanctions, but does anyone want a nuclear war?
And everyone needs to realise China is a major player
A loyal friend to North Korea
And probably the richest country in the world now
There is a new order emerging in the world
It's not America first. It's China!
Thank God that they are a benign superpower
The rest of had better follow their lead

Andrew Aldred

Schooldays

There's a hell of a lot of competition in an all-boys school
It was very difficult to succeed at anything
I wasn't the best at school in a lot of ways
But I wasn't the worst bully, thief, or vandal
Just a misfit and an outcast who didn't want to be there
I spent the last two years running in the lunch-hour
And revising frantically for my "O" levels
I really should have got more than four!
They weren't the happiest days of my life
Just some sort of preparation to join the army
And put my childhood firmly behind me forever

Sorry if I've Caused You Offence

If I've overstepped the mark with anything
Or caused you racial, religious or sexual offence
I'm very sorry I've offended your sensibilities
But I'm a writer and I've got to write about something
And even if I wrote about fluffy bunnies and nothing else
I'd still have some set of people hating me
But even if you think my poems are the rantings of a madman
They still offer some opinion and entertainment
And thank-you so much for bothering to read them

Andrew Aldred

Why?

I can't tell you all the why's and wherefores
But I know all too well this is the way it is
And it has become this way over many centuries
If you can get an education and a trade
You can get a decent job and earn money until you retire
Because you have become rich or you are too ill to work
We hope you will fall in love once or twice
And be able to raise your children the way you want to
If you're sensible you won't waste time rotting in prison
And you'll always see a way around your problems
You can have a happy retirement and go to your grave
And leave someone behind to carry on after you're gone

So Hard Fought

Everything is so hard fought these days
People want to argue over every little detail
You can see it with things like Brexit
And what your children will and won't eat
It is so difficult to get something done
Everyone wants to be in charge
But very few people are fit to take office
And those that do had better beware
Of a fickle public and press
Who will remove them when the slightest thing goes wrong
Life could and should be so much easier
But everybody wants to put themselves first
And that can't be right for a volatile, unstable world

Andrew Aldred

What was he Thinking of?

Now Donald Trump has been openly racist
While the rest of them celebrate Martin Luther King and the civil rights movement
It wasn't enough to field a senator
Who thought the last time America was truly great
Was before the abolition of slavery
Thank God Donald Trump is not coming to this country
Britain can be a model for the rest of the world
A place where people of all factions get on and flourish
Donald Trump has upset North Korea and Iran
And if the president of the U.S. can be openly racist
How will the rest of the American public react?
What was he thinking of? Let's hope he goes soon!

Traffic Incident

Rowena Patel was going to be transferred from Bolton to Harpenden tomorrow. She had been working for Greater Manchester Police force and would be moved to London CID. She had been involved in a routine day in Bolton. There were the usual domestic arguments in Halliwell, and then there was the annoying incident she had not managed to clear up. It concerned a brand-new Jaguar motor car, the pride and joy of her cousin and her cousin's fiancée that had been bumped on a street not too far from where Rowena lived herself. They knew who had done it, some neighbours had reported him. He was an ex-convict, who had not yet owned up to the crime, which was annoyingly minor, but very important to Rowena who had put the man away for a stabbing in Bolton town centre some five years ago.

She had been taken off the case because it involved her family, and all she wanted to do was go around to the guilty man's house, beat the crap out of him and clap him in irons. Her boss had told her this was not the solution to this offence, but she had taken the man's telephone number and intended to use it to get a confession out of him. He was a family man in his fifties who worked on the motorways.

She lived with her mother, her father was five years dead of a heart attack. She packed her few belongings into cardboard boxes and put them into her car ready for tomorrow, when she would drive down to Harpenden, where police accommodation was waiting for her. She had a farewell meal with her mother, who wished her all the best, and let her know she would be missed.

Rowena got out of bed early and began the trip to Harpenden. She left at ten and got there at three-o-clock. She was greeted by her new colleagues, an Asian man and two women, one black and the other white. They decided to go for a meal later that day to introduce Rowena to London.

Rowena went to the flats for the police and made the phone call she had been planning. She rang the ex-convict from a telephone in the flats. She decided to go for the throat and told him she was Manchester Police force and that he had one chance to make a confession because she had evidence against him. He saw that the number was not a Greater Manchester code on his phone and suspected a fake call. He put the phone down on her and she recoiled in disgust, punching the wall. This put her in a bad mood for the rest of the day.

She got ready for the meal in London with her new friends Jonny, Chris and Josie. She dressed to impress, wearing heels and a little black dress, and tying her hair up. They drove down in her car, an old Vauxhall Vectra and went to a posh restaurant in London's West End.

They all drank too much, and the others sympathised with Rowena's story about the ex-convict in Bolton who had got away with damaging her cousin's car. She fancied Jonny, the Asian man, whose real name was Asif, but opted for Jonny as a nickname.

They got into her car and drove home, getting on to the M25, and turning off onto the dual carriageway to Harpenden. Rowena was pre-occupied on the way home, thinking of what else she could have done to get a confession out of the man who had bumped her cousin's car. The alcohol had affected her more than the others, because she did not usually drink. She slotted in behind a car, but did not see two joyriders, who had stolen their car from a supermarket where it had been left with its keys in the ignition. They were going far too fast and had not calculated there would be traffic coming down from the roundabout. They crashed into the back of her car at ninety miles an hour. Both cars spun out of control, hitting the barriers at speed.

Rowena never got to work for London CID, and her colleagues died as did the two joyriders. Rowena became a bitter woman in a wheelchair, who blamed the ex-convict who had bumped her cousin for everything. Pre-occupation with one motoring incident led to another.

The Leprechaun

Harold Doherty lay drunk in the town centre. It was two-o-clock in the morning in the middle of summer. He watched the young man coming down the street on his skateboard through blurred, alcohol sodden eyes. The boy had crept out of his bedroom in the middle of the night to cause mischief. He wore green short pants and a red top. He got off his skateboard and smashed it against a shop window. The window shattered. He walked on and pulled an aerosol of white paint out of his pocket. He sprayed "Fuck the government" on some shop shutters and moving down the road sprayed "Fuck the police" on a nearby wall. He stopped where Harold lay and said, "How are you doing, Dad?". Hearing the sirens, he got on his skateboard, and vanished, leaving Harold with the spray can.

The police came and saw Harold and assumed the obvious. They took Harold to the cells as gently as they could, which was not very gently. He got charged in the morning, but all he could say was that there was a leprechaun there last night who had caused all the upset. Harold was sent to see a psychiatrist, detained under the mental health act and put on a section.

He had worked hard all his life as a labourer and had no formal education. He carried bricks all day and was getting too old for the job, but there was nothing else he was fit for. The psychiatrist put Harold on some pills and he said he could see spacemen everywhere until he got used to them. But he was happy! He did not have to cook meals or work like a dog for a very small wage. All he could not do in hospital was drink like he used to, but the pills sufficed.

Harold served six months at the regional secure unit without incident before he got out. He lives in sheltered accommodation, draws his pension and spends his time in a town-centre pub. He has no worries and thinks the episode with the leprechaun was the best thing that ever happened to him. The psychiatrist wasn't all bad and he has at last got some payback for all his hard work.

Friday Prayers

Darren Littlewood worked as a security guard for a local shopping mall. He was an ex-soldier and was proud of his connections to the military. He attended the local Royal British Legion, he believed in Brexit and he had a deep hatred of the Muslims, who seemed to be taking over in the area where he lived. There was a brand-new mosque and he watched them come out through hate-filled eyes on a Friday after prayers from the pub across the road. Darren had recently got divorced. His wife had taken custody of his only son, Michael Peter, and he was left on his own to hate foreigners, especially Muslims and keep his links with the Army through his Royal British Legion. He felt free to do what he wanted without his wife, who had tried to reason with his extreme beliefs. He thought she had tried to control him and had resented her presence in his life. He was glad to be free of her.

Darren had one or two close friends, also Neo-Nazis and Muslim haters. David and George were members of the local Territorial Army and together they used to dream up plots to do something about the growing Muslim population in their area. David and George had access to some explosives and were able to take advantage of this being Non-commissioned officers. They stole some explosives and made two bombs, one of which they tested in the woods near their town.

They blew it up and to their surprise it did exactly what it was supposed to. They had got the information on how to build a bomb from an Isis website, ironically enough, and they were surprised how well it worked.

It came to the appointed Friday and they planted the bomb outside the mosque where it would be blown up by a signal from a mobile phone once enough people had come out of the building. Darren would make the phone call that blew the bomb up and he sat waiting in the pub across the road. They started to come out and he waited for a while until there were quite a few people there. They had not noticed the child's rucksack, partly because it was dark, which Darren had taken from his son, Michael Peter. He detonated the bomb by phone call and it duly went off. He disguised his delight as he finished his pint and walked out of the pub to the images of mayhem, with blue lights everywhere and injured people.

After the initial chaos, the police cordoned the area off and began their investigation. They found a name-tag reading Michael Peter Littlewood with traces of explosives on it and were able to trace Darren and find out about who he sympathised with and how he had built the bomb. Darren never told on his mates David and George. They remained in the Territorial Army undetected while Darren took the rap, getting a thirty-year jail sentence for a double murder and numerous other charges.

He is still serving his sentence, unable to come to terms with the fact that what he was doing was wrong and that Muslims are here to stay in the United Kingdom.

Oblivion

James swigged the last of the bottle of morphine and waited for the oblivion to take over. He had been diagnosed with cancer of the larynx last year, and the condition had not improved. It had spread to his nose, and he was undergoing his second course of radiotherapy.

Things had been getting too much for James recently. His girlfriend was going bald with the stress of looking after him, and he was unable to drive so she had to go to town every day to get food for them to eat. This left James alone and he went down to the corner shop every day for a bottle of cheap whisky, which he thought helped him cope with his illness. He could no longer smoke, because it hurt his nose and his throat too much. The doctor had been telling him to give up for the past year, but he just had not been able to come to terms with it. He had carried on regardless and this was what had put him in his current situation with an ever-worsening case of cancer. He was physically and mentally unwell, off his head on drink and drugs, and dying of cancer at the same time. His girlfriend could not move out of their house and had vowed to look after James until he was dead or better from his illness, but it was such hard work and he was so difficult.

James' girlfriend came into the house after going shopping that day to see James twitching on the couch. He could not breathe and was having a fit. She called the ambulance and came down to hospital with James, silently hoping that this would be the time and she would be free of her burden. They switched the blue light on and raced off to the hospital.

James remained unconscious and never came back. He died in hospital that night and his girlfriend said it was a relief to them both. He was so uncomfortable with his life and she could not cope. It was not cancer that killed James, although they said he died of natural causes. It was the final trip into oblivion with the morphine that they had given him in the hope of helping him cope with his illness that killed him.

King of the Wasps
The old man sat with his son in the conservatory. The conservatory windows were open, and the room was full of wasps. The old man said to his son, "Kill that one", and pointed to a large wasp by the window. The son took a handkerchief from the table and crushed the wasp. The old man often wondered why the wasps did not sting him, but now he thought he understood. He had provided them with food and a place to live for the last three years. The old man's legs were black with cancer, and he knew he was not long for this world. He asked his son to talk to his daughter and get him an ambulance to take him to hospital to spend the last few days of his life.

The old man had lived in a house surrounded by dense woodland at the bottom of a cul-de-sac. The woodland had been overgrown for some time and this had been put to good use by the old man and his family. There had been two dead bodies in the garden and one in the attic above the house in the last three years. The house had been over-run with wasps every year, because they nested in the dead bodies. The old man and his son were the only people that lived there and the rest of the people they knew called in favours, bringing dead bodies for them to hide and the wasps to eat.

First there was a business associate of one of the old man's friends. They had fallen out and could not resolve who was to take over the company. The old man's friend brought the body in a caravan when he came over to stay, and the body was dumped in the waste ground in front of the house. The old man's son remembered the wasps all over the grass at the front of the house and how he had avoided them with the lawnmower. The next year the nest was empty, and they burned it.

The next body was that of a young girl who had been murdered by one of the old man's sons. She was under-age and had got pregnant to him. She wanted to have the baby and be his wife, but he did not see things the same way. She was stripped naked and put in the attic that Christmas to wait for the wasps the following year. The maggots set into the corpse, and the wasps came in the summer to eat the maggots. She was devoured, and the nest removed the following winter.

For the next body they went back to the garden, where he was buried in the compost heap. This was a man who had attacked one of the old man's sons at a pub in the village. He had been killed with a knife when things got out of hand in a fight and taken back to the old man's house in the middle of the night by car. The old man knew that the wasps never used the same location for their nest twice, and this time the compost heap was used. The man was duly buried and next year he would be compost!

The old man lay in his hospital bed silently. His family came to see him and argued over his dying body about family matters. His organs began to close, and he drifted from one world into the next. He was cremated and put next to his wife, who had died ten years previously. He was quickly forgotten, but the past caught up with his family and friends as they committed more crimes. Maybe in the future, some of their corpses will be eaten by wasps!

Evil Rogue

Paul finished his last pint and permitted himself a wry smile as he had run aground, and this was another town he would have to leave for good. His girlfriend and their daughter would find somebody else to look after them and he was going to be free again. He whistled "David's on the road again" by Manfred Mann and got on a train to Portsmouth where he would work in the fields picking fruit and vegetables during summer before trying to get on X-Factor in the autumn. The whistle blew, and he was on his way, leaving behind a total mess.

Paul was a real-life Del-boy out of "Only fools and horses", but he sold drugs and bought legal goods with the profits, such as clothes and cosmetics, hoping to make it to be a legal trader one day. Recently things had not been going according to plan, and this was why he was on his way down South.

He had come into a large amount of cocaine because there was an excess of the drug in Manchester. He had been able to get it cheaply and sell it on for a lot of effort and a handsome profit. But there was no more to be had after this windfall. Everyone in Ramsbottom had been knocking on Paul's door day and night for weeks, but eventually he had to let them down because he could not get any more. A lot of people were angry with Paul for this, thinking his only function was to provide them with drugs, but Paul had invested the money in some Jeans which he had put his own designer label on. There was "Evil Rogue" for the boys and "Crazy Bitch" for the girls. He had not been able to sell any of them and his girlfriend had taken the lot. They had been left in his garage at his last house.

Paul had been "grassed up" by the drugs community in Ramsbottom and had given a full confession and a lot of information about various people to the police in return for his freedom and a passage out of his hometown.

The train was nearly empty as it pulled out. Paul had taken some cans of beer for the journey, and after a while he decided to go to the toilet. He pressed the button and went in, suddenly being aware of somebody behind him. The stranger put his hand over Paul's mouth with his right hand and thrust a knife under Paul's ribs to his heart with his left. He then waited until the train pulled up at the next station and got off, leaving Paul to be discovered later. When Paul was discovered, he had the words, "Evil Rogue" written on his forehead in biro. The jeans did quite well when somebody got around to selling them.

www.ingramcontent.com/pod-product-compliance
Lightning Source LLC
Chambersburg PA
CBHW031935080426
42734CB00007B/699